Color!

Meditation Mandala Coloring

Book 1

Deb Gilbert

Heller Brothers Publishing

Title: Color! Meditation Mandala Coloring, Book I
Author: Deb Gilbert
Published by: Heller Brothers Publishing
Copyright © 2016 by Deb Gilbert
Photo Credits: OlgaDrozd@depositphotos.com
First Edition, 2016
Published in USA

ISBN 978-1-944678-07-4

ISBN 978-1-944678-07-4   US$7.99
50799>
9 781944 678074

This Coloring Book Belongs To:

_____

Color!

Meditation Mandala Coloring

Book I

Notes from Deb

I started coloring due to a fall that resulted in a chronic condition--sciatica. For seven months, I was unable to do much more than sit in a recliner or sleep. To keep my attention away from the constant pain level of 9 or 10, I colored.

It relaxed me, gave me time to think pleasant thoughts, and allowed me a respite from worrying about my condition. While overwhelmed by chronic pain and the drugs that doctors prescribed, I found many hours of peace just by coloring.

I had my pens and pencils carefully within reach. I used a large postal envelope behind my pages so that my pens did not bleed onto the next page. I imagine a sheet of paper would work well for this, too.

As I continued my healing, I found that coloring had become my relaxing habit. I gradually began being able to walk and to resume many of my regular day-to-day activities. However, each evening I was sore and wiped out. It is this child-like activity that keeps me focused and gives me hours of pleasure.

I design coloring books for everyone, but I keep in mind my fellow chronic pain sufferers and wish them many hours of active engagement and peace.

> **"We will be more successful in all our endeavors if we can
> let go of the habit of running all the time,
> and take little pauses to relax and re-center ourselves.
> And we'll also have a lot more joy in living."**
> **----Thich Nhat Hanh**

Date Completed: _____
Media Used:_____
_____
_____
Notes: _____
_____
_____
_____
_____

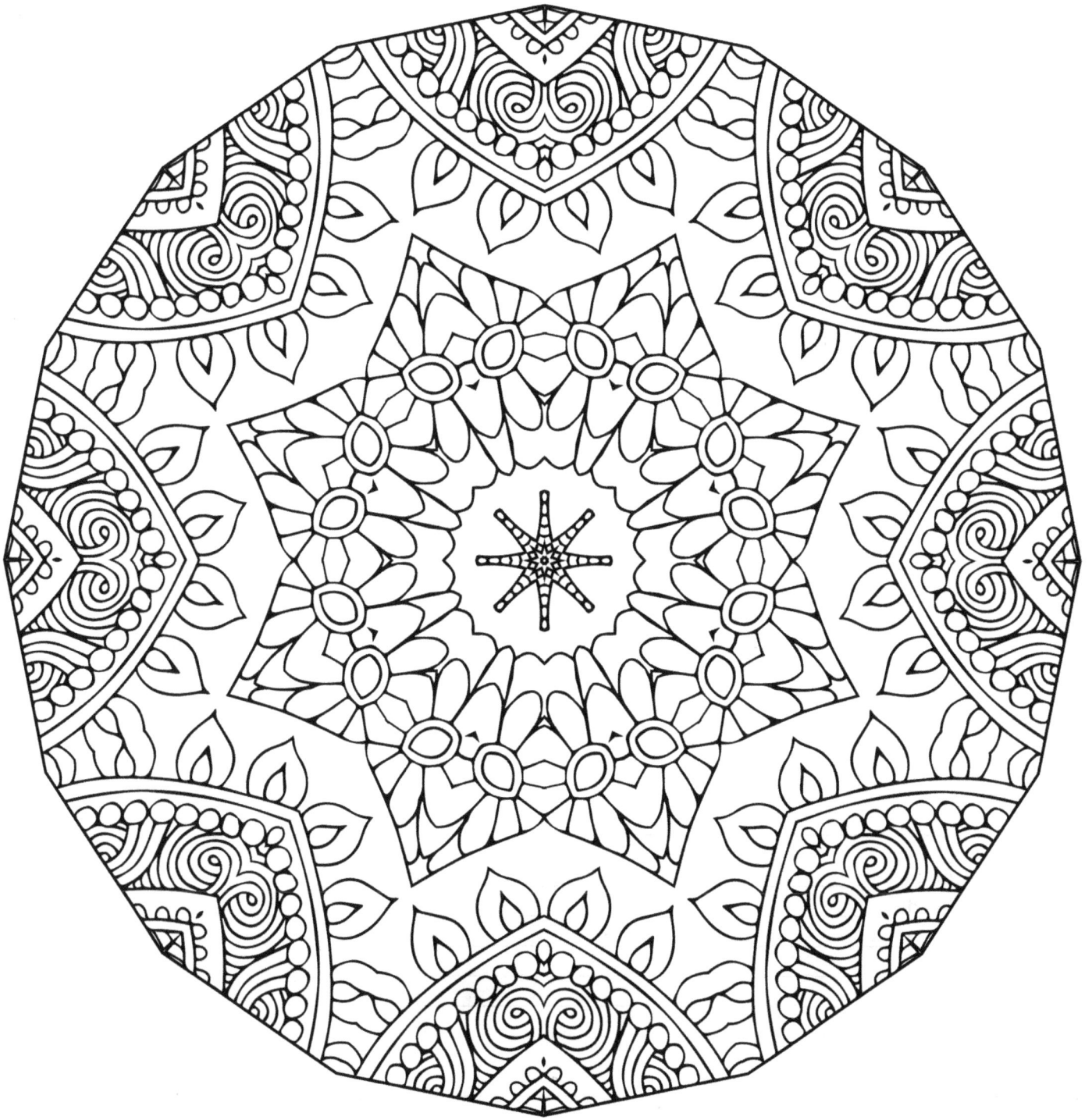

Date Completed: _____

Media Used:_____

_____

_____

Notes: _____

_____

_____

_____

_____

Date Completed: _____

Media Used: _____

_____

_____

Notes: _____

_____

_____

_____

_____

Date Completed: _____

Media Used:_____

_____
_____

Notes: _____

_____
_____
_____
_____
_____

Date Completed: _____
Media Used:_____
_____
_____
Notes: _____
_____
_____
_____
_____

Date Completed: _____

Media Used:_____

_____

_____

Notes: _____

_____

_____

_____

_____

Date Completed: _____

Media Used:_____

_____

_____

Notes: _____

_____

_____

_____

_____

Date Completed: _____

Media Used:_____

_____

_____

Notes: _____

_____

_____

_____

_____

_____

Date Completed: _____

Media Used:_____

_____

_____

Notes: _____

_____

_____

_____

_____

Date Completed: _____

Media Used: _____

_____

_____

Notes: _____

_____

_____

_____

_____

Date Completed: _____

Media Used:_____

_____

_____

Notes: _____

_____

_____

_____

_____

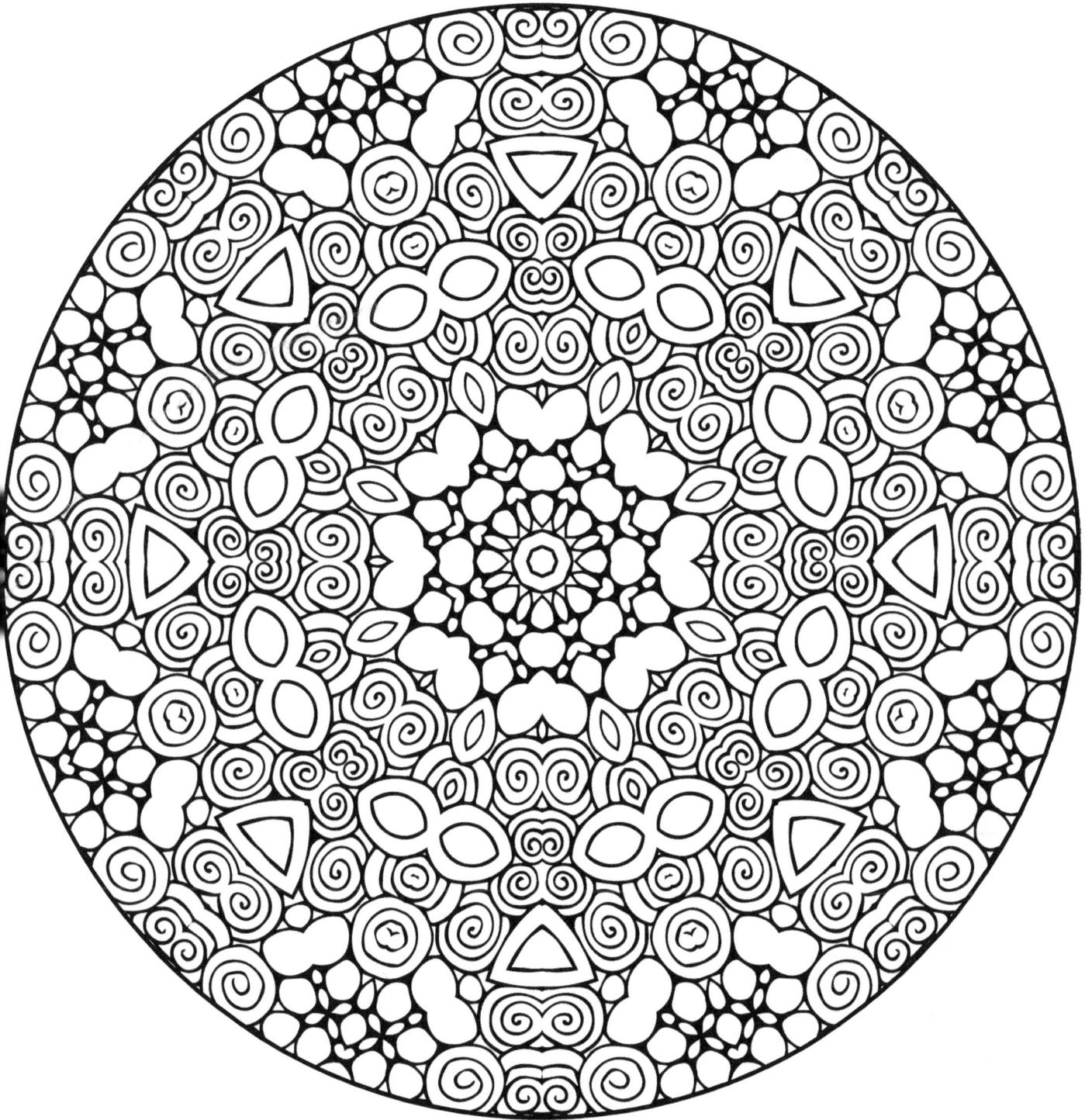

Date Completed: _____

Media Used:_____

_____

_____

Notes: _____

_____

_____

_____

_____

Date Completed: _____
Media Used:_____
_____
_____
Notes: _____
_____
_____
_____
_____

Date Completed: _____

Media Used:_____

_____

_____

Notes: _____

_____

_____

_____

_____

Date Completed: _____

Media Used:_____

_____

_____

Notes: _____

_____

_____

_____

_____

Date Completed: _____

Media Used:_____

_____

_____

Notes: _____

_____

_____

_____

_____

Date Completed: _____

Media Used:_____

_____

_____

Notes: _____

_____

_____

_____

_____

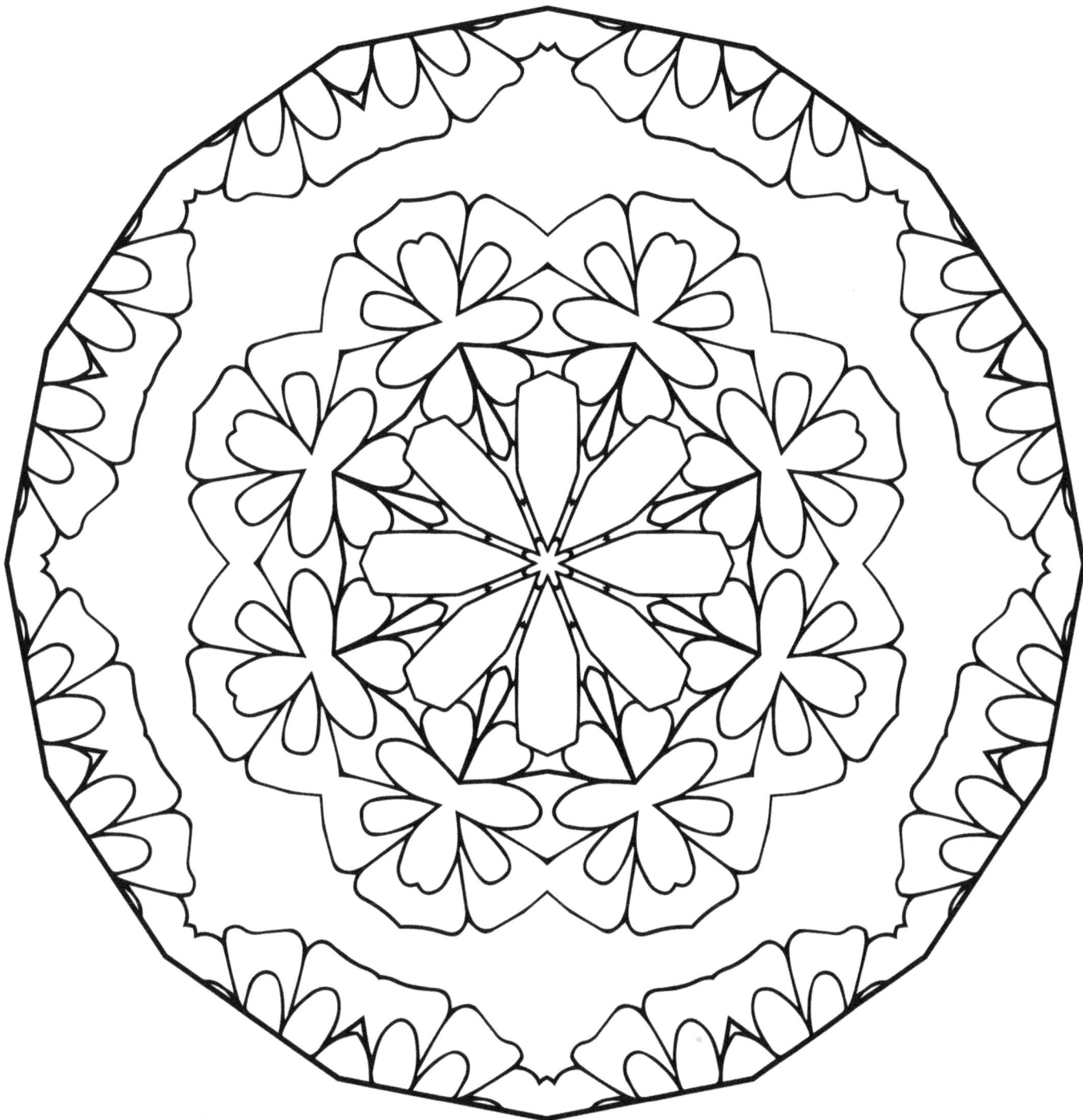

Date Completed: _____

Media Used:_____

_____

_____

Notes: _____

_____

_____

_____

_____

Date Completed: _____

Media Used:_____

_____

_____

Notes: _____

_____

_____

_____

_____

Date Completed: _____
Media Used:_____
_____
_____
Notes: _____
_____
_____
_____
_____
_____

Date Completed: _____

Media Used:_____

_____

_____

Notes: _____

_____

_____

_____

_____

Date Completed: _____

Media Used:_____

_____

_____

Notes: _____

_____

_____

_____

_____

_____

Date Completed: _____

Media Used:_____

_____

_____

Notes: _____

_____

_____

_____

_____

Date Completed: _____

Media Used:_____

_____

_____

Notes: _____

_____

_____

_____

_____

Date Completed: _____

Media Used:_____

_____

_____

Notes: _____

_____

_____

_____

_____

_____

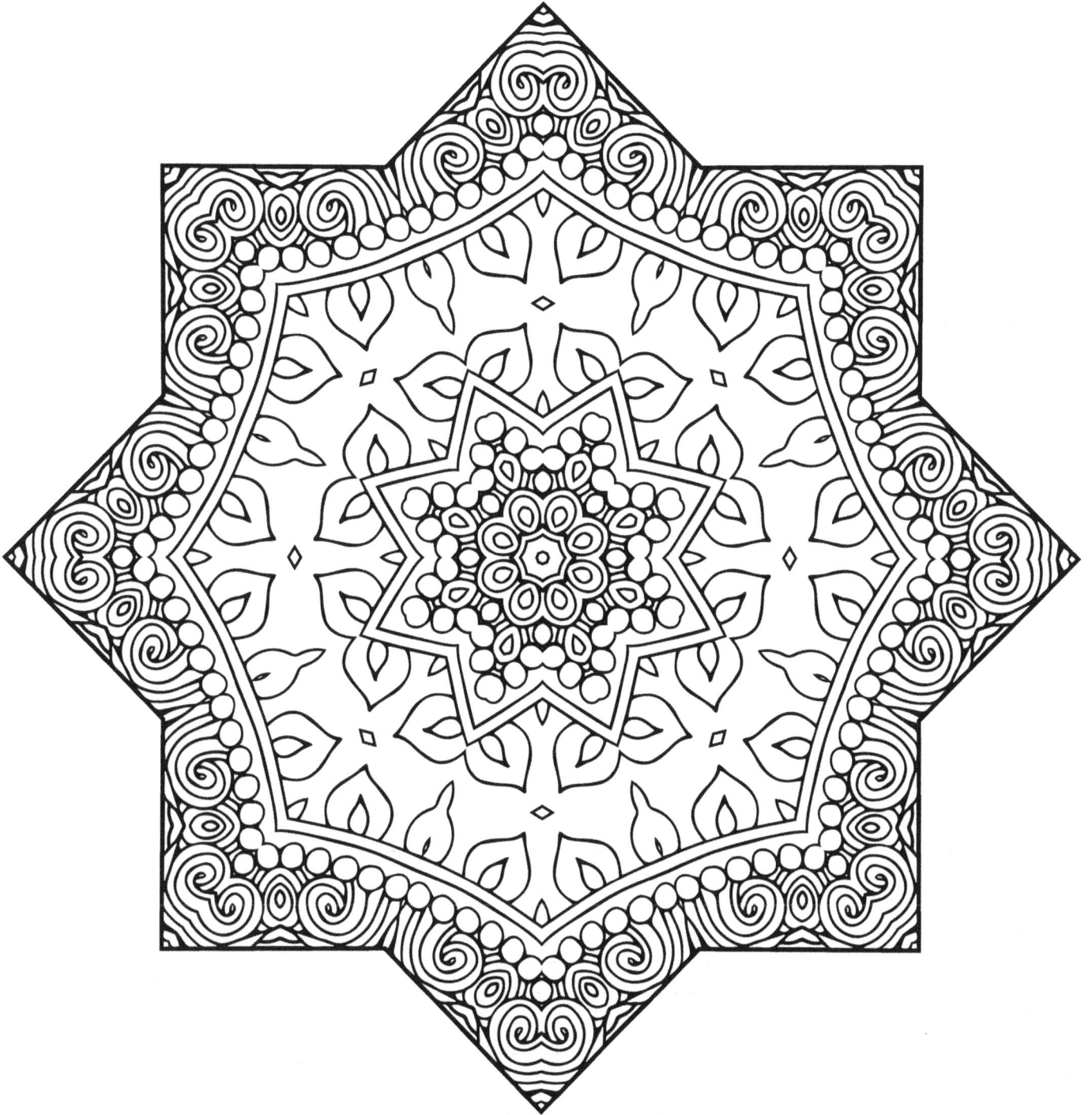

Date Completed: _____

Media Used:_____

_____

_____

Notes: _____

_____

_____

_____

_____

_____

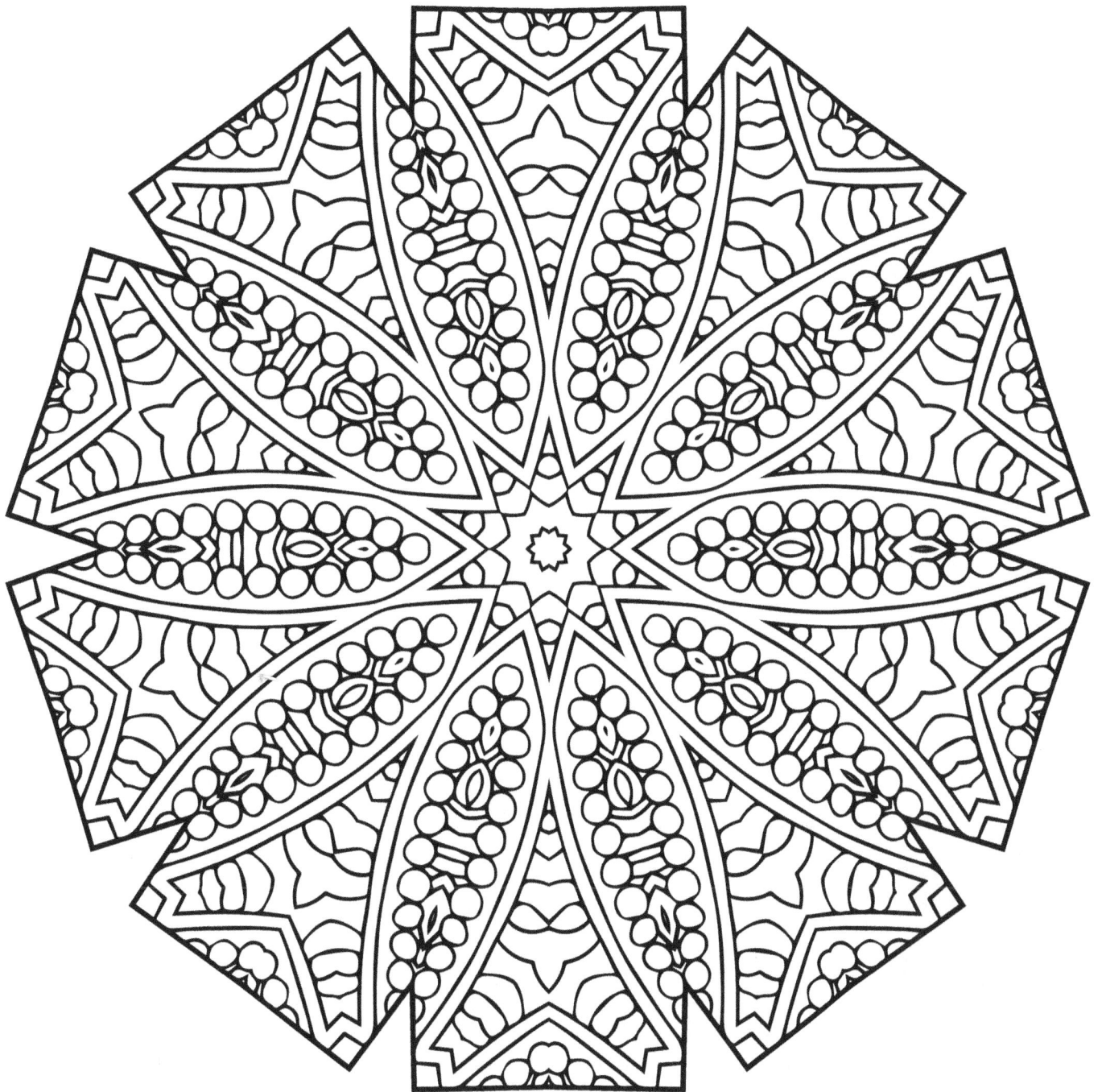

Date Completed: _____

Media Used:_____

_____

_____

Notes: _____

_____

_____

_____

_____

Date Completed: _____

Media Used: _____

_____

_____

Notes: _____

_____

_____

_____

_____

_____

Date Completed: _____

Media Used:_____

_____

_____

Notes: _____

_____

_____

_____

_____

Date Completed: _____

Media Used:_____

_____

_____

Notes: _____

_____

_____

_____

_____

Date Completed: _____

Media Used:_____

_____

_____

Notes: _____

_____

_____

_____

_____

Date Completed: _____
Media Used:_____
_____
_____
Notes: _____
_____
_____
_____
_____

Date Completed: _____

Media Used:_____

_____

_____

Notes: _____

_____

_____

_____

_____

_____

Date Completed: _____
Media Used:_____
_____
_____
Notes: _____
_____
_____
_____
_____

About the Author

Dr. Deb Gilbert has been working from home since 2007 and is an online professor of education, research, and leadership. She has been involved in public schools and higher education for over 25 years and has a passion for promoting literacy. In addition, she relaxes by coloring and designing coloring books for adults.

For more information on Deb Gilbert, please join her at
www.hellerbrotherspublishing.com
and on Facebook at:
https://www.facebook.com/coloringbooksforhealing

www.ingramcontent.com/pod-product-compliance
Lightning Source LLC
Chambersburg PA
CBHW081240020426
42331CB00013B/3242